FITTER, FASTER, FUNNIER FOOTBALL!

Michael Cox

ILLUSTRATED BY MIGUEL FRANCISCO

A & C BLACK
AN IMPRINT OF BLOOMSBURY
LONDON NEW DELHI NEW YORK SYDNEY

Contents

So What's So Funny About The Football World Cup?

We all know that the international competition known as the FIFA World Cup is an awe-inspiring soccer spectacle in which world-class football teams battle for glory. But did you know that it's also the setting for absolutely hundreds of weird, wonderful and wildly hilarious moments! In this book you will discover . . .

Which player passed out after his delighted team jumped on him to celebrate his goal?

Whose team captain played with his specs on in the 1938 World Cup final?

Which 1970 World Cup striker later worked as a window cleaner with an advertising sign that said, 'He misses no corners!'

How a team's physio was rendered unconscious when he ran onto the field to treat an injured player?

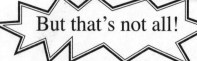

But that's not all!

Find out if you've got what it takes to be a World Cup soccer superhero, by completing two hilarious questionnaires: how to score a winning World Cup goal with the perfect penalty kick; and how to be a dynamic dribbler, superb shooter, heroic header, dauntless defender and gutsy goalie.

And if that's not enough to keep you glued to your football stadium seat, there are also World Cup quizzes to do and, brain teasers for you to try. Plus lots, lots more!

So what are you waiting for! Lace up your footie boots, slot in your shin pads and slip on your shorts! Then it's . . .

TIME TO KICK OFF!

1 FANTASTIC FOOTBALL

HOW IT ALL STARTED

Football officially began in England in 1848 when the first ever rules were laid down for the game at Cambridge University. But all sorts of versions of footy have been played for yonks longer than that. Some matches involved teams of a thousand players with goals ten miles apart, whilst others, such as 'Calcio' first played in the 16th century in Italy, involved a mere 27 players per team and took place in a giant sandpit.

The footballs themselves have also varied a lot. Early ones were stuffed with materials ranging from fur, moss, grass and sawdust to caribou hair and, quite often, weren't particularly round. However, the 'Jabulani' balls, which were used in the 2010 World Cup in South Africa, were claimed by their makers to be the 'roundest footballs ever'. The 'least round football ever' was probably the one used in one of the first ever matches to be played in

England. In this little 7th century 'kick-around', victorious Saxon warriors used the head of a defeated Viking prince as their ball (fortunately for him, it was no longer attached to his body).

HOW TO PLAY 'SHROVETIDE' FOOTBALL, ASHBOURNE STYLE

Even though they eventually gave up booting around the decapitated heads of Scandiwegian noblemen, many of these old soccer games continued to be extremely violent. And still are! For instance, the 'footbrawl' match which has been played on Pancake Day for at least eight hundred years in the Derbyshire town of Ashbourne. Read on to get an idea of how the modern game has come on since then.

1 Split your players into two teams: the Up'Ards (players who live north of the river) and the Down'Ards (players who live south of the river).

2 Don't worry about limiting your teams to 11 men each. Have as many as 100, if you want to!

3 Your goals are mill stones. Set them three miles apart, each one in the river. Yes, you're going to get wet. In fact, you may well end up playing your entire game in the river!

4 Suggest to the local shopkeepers that they board up their windows as, come 'kick-off' things around the town, will be getting a bit lively.

5 Kick off at two in the afternoon and continue playing until ten at night - yes, a mere eight hours!

6 Start your game by appointing a 'turner upper', that's the person who stands on the raised 'plinth' then lobs the ball towards the waiting mob, sorry the waiting players.

7 Rather than scoring by putting the ball into your opponents' goal, you must attempt to get it to your own goal post, then tap it three times.

8 You can kick, carry or throw the ball, but you must not hide it down your trousers, in a bag or under your coat.

9 You must not hop on a bus with the ball or sneak into your car and drive it the three miles back to your goal.

10 Rough play is allowed but you must not go as far as actually murdering your opponents (this would get you a red card, not to mention life imprisonment).

2 THE FITTER FASTER FUNNIER WORLD CUP TIMELINE

FEARSOME FOOTY FACTS!

1930
First ever World Cup tournament, Uruguay
Winners: Uruguay

⚽ The crowd for Romania v Peru at the 1930 finals was a whopping... 300!

⚽ 4,444 fans saw France's Lucien Laurent score the first ever World Cup goal against Mexico.

⚽ Alex Villaplane, France's captain in that first ever 1930 World Cup match against Mexico, was killed 15 years later for collaborating with the Germans in World War Two.

⚽ Uruguayan forward, Hector Castro, played with only one hand because he had accidentally sawn off the other one whilst doing a bit of woodwork.

When the Bolivian team ran onto the pitch, the letters on their shirts read as:

The crowd looked on, puzzled. Then the team lined up properly and they saw it read:

1934

Host country: Italy
Winners: Italy

⚽ Thirty-two countries applied for 16 places in the finals so the first qualifying competition was introduced.

This beats drawing straws.

⚽ It was reported that Italian Fascist dictator Benito Mussolini told his national team,

"WIN… OR DIE!"

"Vincere o morire!"

1938

Host country: France
Winners: Italy (again!)

⚽ Argentina wanted to host the World Cup as they thought it was time for South America's turn again. However, France got the honour so Argentina and Uruguay refused to turn up to the tournament.

⚽ Spain didn't play either because they were busy having a civil war.

⚽ Nor did Austria as their next door neighbours, Germany, had just invaded them and taken them over.

1950

Host country: Brazil
Winners: Uruguay

⚽ After taking a 12 year break, the footballing countries of the world finally got back together for another World Cup tournament in South America.

⚽ England didn't really enjoy it much as they were humiliated in a 1-0 defeat by soccer newbies, the USA.

1954

Host country: Switzerland
Winners: West Germany

⚽ At the Uruguay v England match, Uruguay got a free kick. It was reported that the moment the referee wasn't looking a cheating Uruguayan player picked up the ball then booted it down the field. An instant later, the Uruguayans scored.

1958

Host country: Sweden
Winners: Brazil

⚽ In the final of this tournament, Brazil beat Sweden 5-2. Two of these goals were scored by 17-year-old boy-wonder, Edson Arantes Nascimento. Overwhelmed by his achievement, Edson, who would go on to be known as Pele, burst into tears at the end of the game.

⚽ But this was only the beginning. It was reported that he managed to score another astonishing 1,088 goals in his amazing footballing career and is regarded by many as the best footballer ever.

1962

Host country: Chile
Winners: Brazil

(again!)

⚽ To make sure no children missed the fun, every school in Chile was shut down for the entire tournament.

⚽ The footballs supplied by the Chileans kept going shapeless and flat so the matches were started with a Chilean ball, which was replaced with a good quality ball at half time.

1966

Host country: England
Winners: England

⚽ After it was reported that England manager Alf Ramsey described the Argentinian players as behaving like animals in their match against his team, the secretary of the British Dog Owners Association complained that this comment was unfair to both dogs and their humans.

⚽ England went on to win the World Cup 4-2 in their thrilling match against Germany.

1970

Host country: Mexico
Winners: Brazil

⚽ Brazilian superstar, Pele, headed the ball at the net and yelled . . .

GOAL!

but English goalie, Gordon Banks saved it.

'AS SAFE AS THE BANKS OF ENGLAND'

soon became a popular catch phrase!

1974

Host country: West Germany
Winners: West Germany

⚽ The start of the tournament was apparently delayed because the Germans forgot to set out the corner posts (so why didn't they just use jumpers?).

⚽ Belgium won their first ever world cup match, 40 years after first competing in the tournament in 1930!

⚽ The West Germans did go on to win, despite being separated from East Germany after World War Two and therefore only had half the population to pick their team from!

1978
Host country: Argentina
Winners: Argentina

⚽ Apparently the Scots complained that their training pitch was so bad even the cows wouldn't eat the grass on it.

⚽ In the final, the Argentinians may have used the trick of delaying their entrance onto the pitch which left their opponents, Holland to be booed and jeered by the massive home crowd. This unsettled the Holland team who went on to lose 3-1.

1982
Host country: Spain
Winners: Italy

⚽ The Kuwaiti team threatened to abandon their game against France because someone in the crowd had whistled which they thought had come from the referee, causing them to stop playing. At this point, their opponents, France, had made the most of the opportunity and scored, leaving the Kuwaitis feeling very miffed! However, the referee eventually disallowed the goal and, with a little encouragement from Prince Fahid of Kuwait, the Kuwaitis agreed to continue playing.

1986
Host country: Mexico
Winners: Argentina

⚽ Diego Maradona scored both goals in Argentina's 2-1 victory over England in the finals. The second of them was considered to be a brilliant piece of football by everyone who saw it. But, despite the fact that he scored the first by actually punching it into the goal, the referee allowed it. It was later reported that Maradona claimed it was scored 'A LITTLE WITH THE HEAD OF MARADONA AND A LITTLE WITH THE HAND OF GOD'.

⚽ The international governing body of football, FIFA prohibited shirt swapping because they did not want players to 'bare their chests' on the field.

1990

Host country: Italy
Winners: West Germany

"We got here. But I don't know how."

⚽ When England reached the semi-final their manager Bobby Robson reportedly said,

⚽ When English player Paul 'Gazza' Gascoigne was given a yellow card denying him a potential place in the World Cup final, he burst into tears. But it didn't matter anyway, because England lost on penalties. As they would do a few more times!

1994

Host country: United States of America
Winners: Brazil

yet again!

⚽ Apparently, 20 American spectators walked out of the stadium when Germany scored against Bolivia. Maybe these spectators thought a football match is over as soon as someone scores a goal.

1998

Host country: France
Winners: France

⚽ Tickets for the tournament were like gold – 15 million English fans called the ticket hot-line but hundreds of them forgot to add the extra numbers for calling France and ended up talking to a woman called Mrs Brown who lived in Southend!

⚽ During England's match against Argentina, David Beckham was fouled by an Argentinian. In response Beckham kicked out at him and was sent off. It was reported that effigies of the Manchester United player were burned in the streets but a church in Mansfield, Nottinghamshire put up a notice saying:

'GOD FORGIVES – EVEN DAVID BECKHAM!'

2002

Host country: South Korea and Japan
Winners: Brazil *again!!*

⚽ A World Cup record was set when the youngest ever World Cup player, Souleymane Maman, a mere 13-year-old slip-of-a-lad, played for Togo against Zambia in the 2001 qualifiers.

2006

Host country: Germany
Winners: Italy

⚽ England reached the quarter-finals to play against Portugal.

⚽ England's Scandiwegian manager, Sven-Göran Eriksson said,

> "It will NOT be my last day in charge. I'm certain of that. It's not going to go wrong. We will WIN!"

England lost on penalty shootouts.

2010

Host country: South Africa
Winners: Spain

⚽ Fans blew long horns known as vuvuzelas throughout the matches and everyone complained about the horrible noise they made — apart from the vuvuzela blowers!

⚽ South Africa were knocked out in the first round of the tournament. This was the first time this had ever happened to a host country.

AND iF YOU HAVEN'T ALREADY WORKED it OUT ...

The winners so far, are:

BRAZIL: 5 World Cups

ITALY: 4 World Cups

WEST GERMANY: 3 World Cups

ARGENTINA: 2 World Cups

URUGUAY: 2 World Cups

ENGLAND: 1 World Cup

FRANCE: 1 World Cup

SPAIN: 1 World Cup

3 WORLD CUP SOCCER SUPER-STARS

GUESS THE SOCCER SUPER-STAR

How well do you know your footballing super-heroes? Read the clues below and see if you can figure out who they're describing!

1 As a child he played barefoot in the streets with a ball made from a sock stuffed with paper. He only played 14 World Cup games but still managed to score an amazing 12 goals during those games and also won three World Cups with his team. Once, when he was taking a free kick, the stadium announcer was so confident this super-star would score that he announced that he was about to put away his 1,000th goal. And of course, he did!

2 This football legend started playing football at the age of eight with a youth team in 1954, against the wishes of his dad, who disliked football. He won two European footballer-of-the-year awards, three Euro Cups and captained his country's team in their World Cup victory in 1974. He also invented the position of 'sweeper' in modern football. As a result of his phenomenal leadership skills, fans gave him the nickname of **'Der Kaiser'** which means **'The Emperor'**.

3 This left-footed footballer scored 83 goals in 84 international matches. Having been an army officer he was nicknamed the **Galloping Major**. It's said that his family were so poor that they could only afford to buy him a shoe for his right foot. So in order to save wear and tear on his beloved new footwear item he would only use his left foot for kicking. He led his international team to a world record of 32 consecutive games without a single defeat.

4 His nickname is **'Der bomber'**. He scored ten goals in six games playing for his country at the 1970 World Cup. This included hat-tricks in their games against Bulgaria and Peru. He also held the record for overall goals total in the World Cup for more than 30 years.

5 This soccer super-star dropped out of school when he was 11 so that he could concentrate on developing his footy skills and he was signed to his first club at the age of 12. At the 2002 World Cup he scored eight goals in seven games. He was also the FIFA World player of the year in 1996 and 1997 and led his team to two World Cup Championships. His superb soccer skills have earned him the nickname **'the Phenomenon'**.

Answers

1) Edison Arantes do Nascimento better known as 'Pelé' (born 21st October, 1940)

2) Franz Anton Beckenbauer (born 11th September, 1945)

3) Ferenc Puskas (1927 - 2006)

4) Gerhard 'Gerd' Muller (born 3rd November, 1945)

5) Ronaldo Luiz Nazário de Lima commonly known as Ronaldo (born 22nd September, 1976)

HAVE YOU GOT WHAT IT TAKES TO BE A WORLD CUP HERO?

Do you think you've got what it takes to be an all star World Cup hero? Take this test and find out!

PART ONE: QUESTIONS ABOUT YOU

1. SKILL

You are in a perfect position to score and your team mate delivers you a perfect pass. Do you...

a) blast the ball, then watch proudly as it sails into the back of the net

b) fall over the ball

c) take a wild kick at the ball, miss it completely then watch as your football boot sails into the back of the net

2. FITNESS

After being on the pitch for 30 very energetic minutes are you...

a) still absolutely full of energy and determination

b) pretending you've had a heart attack so those kind men with the stretcher will take you somewhere warm and comfy for a nice cup of tea

c) passed out in an oxygen tent

3. ATTITUDE

Your team is losing 2-0 in the 25th minute. Do you...

a) yell, "Come on lads, we're gonna pull out all the stops and win this game no matter what!"

b) tell them that, "all is lost!" and that you should all pack up and go home

b) begin to sob uncontrollably

4. TEAMWORK

Your team mate has brilliantly dribbled the ball past six members of the other team and is now about to blast it into the net. Do you...

a) put yourself in a position where you can give him maximum support should anything go wrong

b) run alongside him telling him that his hair looks rubbish

c) block him so that you can get the ball off him then take the perfect shot at goal

5. SELF DISCIPLINE

The referee is booking you for a foul on a member of the opposition. Do you...

a) accept the booking and apologise for your bad behaviour

b) tell the referee you know where he lives

c) pick up the ball and run off with it

PART TWO: QUESTIONS ABOUT YOUR KNOWLEDGE OF THE GAME

1. What does a team's captain wear to signify his role?

a) an armband

b) a really big hat with 'THE BOSS' written on it

c) chain mail

2. **The horizontal bar across the top of the goal is known as...**
a) the cross bar
b) the mainmast
c) the juice bar

3. **When a player scores three goals in a match it is known as a...**
a) hat-trick
b) circus trick
c) hat stand

4. **The penalty area is also known as...**
a) the box
b) the patio
c) the vuvuzela

5. **The defender whose job it is to protect the space between the goalkeeper and the rest of the defence is known as...**
a) the sweeper
b) the hairdresser
c) Simon

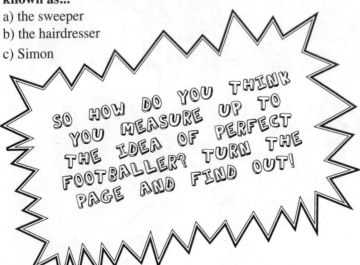

SO HOW DO YOU THINK YOU MEASURE UP TO THE IDEA OF PERFECT FOOTBALLER? TURN THE PAGE AND FIND OUT!

HOW DID YOU SCORE?

Work out how may times you answered A, how many times you answered B, and how many times you answered C. Then read your results on the next page:

IF YOU ANSWERED MAINLY A

Well you certainly have the skill, temperament and knowledge of the game to put you in the running. But remember, there are thousands more out there just like you, so you're going to have to go that extra mile to prove you have the super skills and commitment that make a truly great footballer.

IF YOU ANSWERED MAINLY B

Hmm, your skills and attitude are perhaps not all they should be. Maybe you should just restrict your involvement with soccer to being a spectator who is keen to fill those yawning gaps in their footballing knowledge.

IF YOU ANSWERED MAINLY C

You shouldn't be allowed within five miles of a football pitch or stadium. Your best idea would to be to stick to other hobbies such as train-spotting or making model castles from empty washing-up liquid bottles!

How Not to Lose Your Place in a World Cup Team

A player may well have the talent and dedication to get themselves a place on a World Cup team but, having secured it, they have to make sure they don't lose it by doing something silly, like this bunch did!

1. DON'T BE A 'BUTTER FINGERS' (ESPECIALLY IF YOU'RE A GOALIE!)

Just before his team's game against Ireland in the 2002 World Cup in South Korea and Japan, Spanish goalkeeper, Santiago Canizares, dropped a bottle of aftershave in the bathroom sink at his hotel. The bottle shattered and a big piece of glass sliced into his foot and severed a tendon in his big toe. He was rushed to hospital for emergency treatment and as a consequence of his clumsiness he missed the entire tournament.

2. STICK TO WHAT YOU'RE GOOD AT!

Brazil's captain and midfield player at the 2002 World Cup, Emerson Ferreira da Rosa, decided to go in goal while his team were playing a practice match just before the tournament began. Diving to save the ball, he dislocated his shoulder and spent the rest of the competition watching from the sidelines.

3. GET YOUR DIARY ORGANISED!

Argentine Captain Manuel Ferreira missed their 1930 game against Mexico because he had to pop back to Argentina to take a law exam.

4. DON'T GO 'ABSENT WITHOUT LEAVE'!

It was widely reported that for eight weeks before the 1930 World Cup tournament the management of the Uruguayan team confined them to a secret hideaway so that they could give 100% concentration to their crucial preparations. However, the Uruguayan goalkeeper, Antonio Mazzali, tried to sneak out of the hideaway so that he could pay a visit to his family. He was caught and instantly kicked off his team.

5. DON'T LEAVE YOUR REGISTRATION CARD BEHIND!

England's opening match against Uruguay in the 1966 World Cup finals tournament was held up because seven England players had left their registration cards back at the team hotel. A police motorcyclist was sent to get them.

6. BEWARE OF LARGE DEER!

Admittedly it wasn't at a World Cup but this one's still worth a mention. During the 1970s, Norway defender Svein Grondalen apparently ran slap bang into a moose while he was out jogging, sustaining injuries that forced him to withdraw from an international match.

JUST FOR LUCK!

To ensure you keep your place on the team and play brilliantly you might like to try a few good luck charms. World Cup footballers can be a very superstitious lot indeed and many go through all sorts of rigmaroles to ensure that luck stays with them during their big games. Here are just a few of the routines and rituals they're supposed to have carried out.

SERGIO'S 'WEE' HABIT

Apparently before a penalty, team mate Argentinian goalkeeper, Sergio Goycochea, always did a wee on the pitch to bring himself good luck.

HOW TO GIVE THE OPPOSITION A RIGHT 'PASTING'

It is said that before his team's first match of the 1986 World Cup, Argentina's manager, Carlos Bilardo borrowed some toothpaste from one of his players. They went on to win the game so, thinking it might bring his team luck (not to mention saving him money), he continued to use borrowed toothpaste for the rest of the tournament.

SUPERSTITION, COULD IT BE NOBBY'S HOBBY?

England mid-fielder Nobby Stiles was very superstitious indeed. Before a match he would apparently always get changed in the same order...

1 Put on his shirt and shorts

2 Grease his boots, on the inside

3 Soak his feet in hot water

4 Put on his socks and boots

5 Take off his shirt and rub his chest and legs with olive oil

6 Put his shirt back on

7 Tie his boot-laces

8 Grease his hands and face

9 Take off his specs and put in his contact lenses

10 Take out his false teeth

11 Comb his hair

JOHN TERRY'S GOOD LUCK ROUTINE

Perhaps this England ex-captain is even more superstitious than Nobby. It has been reported that before a game he always...

A Listened to the same CD in his car on the way to the match

B Parked his car in exactly the same spot every time

C Sat on the same seat if he and his fellow players were travelling to the match on the team coach

D Tied the tapes that hold up his socks three times

E Cut the tubular grip for his shin pads exactly the same length

F Used the same pair of 'lucky' shin pads – apparently he did this for ten years but then he lost them at an away game in Barcelona

PELE'S BAD PATCH

After giving away his match shirt to a fan in a fit of generosity, Pele started to go through a really bad patch in his playing so apparently he asked a pal to track down the shirt and get it back for him in the hope that his form would return. Supposedly a week later the pal handed the 'lucky' shirt to Pele who began wearing it again and immediately returned to top form. However, what the pal didn't tell Pele was that he hadn't bothered tracking down the lost shirt but had just given him one that looked like it.

LAURENT'S BALD PATCH

During the 1998 World Cup in his home country, French centre-back, Laurent Blanc, kissed the shiny bald patch of his goalkeeper before every match. And it worked: they won the World Cup! Well it was maybe that or the fact they all played exceptionally well.

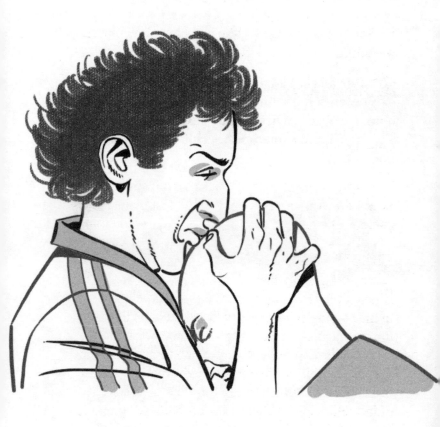

THE WORLD CUP'S WEIRDEST MOMENTS

PART ONE

After all that edge-of-your-seat, soccer superhero intensity, it's time for a little break. Read on to discover the first of our startling, supremely silly, weird and sometimes, seriously scary, soccer moments...

1 As part of the opening ceremony of the 1994 USA World Cup, celebrity soul singer (and non-pro footballer), Diana Ross was to take a penalty, which the goalkeeper would let in as previously planned. Nevertheless, despite the goalie being very 'co-operative' she still missed the goal by miles.

2 Proudly jogging out of the tunnel at the start of the 1950 Brazil v Yugoslavia match, Rajko Mitic ran straight into a metal girder and promptly jogged back in. Ten minutes later he jogged out again, this time with a bandage around his head.

3 When the 1970 World Cup striker, Jeff Astle, retired from football he set up a window-cleaning business. His advertising sign proudly proclaimed:

'JEFF ASTLE NEVER MISSES THE CORNERS!'

4 Swiss centre-forward Poldi Kielholz scored three goals in two matches at the 1934 finals wearing his spectacles. The Dutch East Indies (now Indonesia) side, which appeared at the 1938 World Cup finals was captained by a doctor, Acmad Nawir, who also wore his glasses during the games.

5 American physiotherapist, Jack Coll, was rendered unconscious during the 1930 semi-final against Argentina when he ran onto the field to treat an injured player. He dropped his bag and a bottle of chloroform broke inside it. Poor Jack was instantly flat on his back, knocked out by the chemical's fumes!

6 It was reported that Scotland wore thick wool jerseys with long sleeves and buttoned collars for their match against Uruguay at the 1954 finals. Unfortunately, the temperature was in the thirties. The Scottish team had assumed Switzerland was cold because it had mountains. The Uruguayans wore light V-necked shirts with short sleeves. The Scots lost 7-0.

7 Apparently during the 2006 World Cup, English journalists played 'Sven Bingo'. They had a list of England manager, Sven-Göran Eriksson's most wacky words and phrases. The moment the Swede uttered linguistic gems such as, "first half good, second half not so good" or referred to his key striker, Wayne Rooney, as, "Wine Roney" during his press conferences, they ticked them off on their 'Sven Bingo' score cards.

8 Two players in the 1986 World Cup England team were both called Gary Stevens. Whenever they were on the pitch, the fans would sing, "There's only two Gary Stevens! There's only two Gary Stevens!".

9 Belgium's Jean Langenus refereed the 1930 Argentina v Uruguay final wearing plus fours, a tie and a deerstalker hat.

47

5 THE ONION BAG

HAVE YOU GOT WHAT IT TAKES TO BE A WORLD CLASS GOALIE?

One of the most demanding and scariest jobs in World Cup football is playing in goal, or the 'onion bag' as players refer to it. Your every move is, quite literally, being watched and evaluated by billions of armchair soccer 'experts', not to mention your manager, fans and team mates. Walter Zenga holds the record of longest unbeaten goalkeeper in World Cup history and played 517 minutes – almost six games – without letting in a single goal!

Take the quiz below and find out if you could be a world class goalie!

1. A good goalie must have...
a) excellent handling skills
b) a really massive hairdo
c) telescopic arms

2. When a goalkeeper is organising a line of players to defend against a free kick it is known as...
a) building a wall
b) building a conservatory
c) being a big bossy-boots

3. Good goalkeepers should be able to accurately pass the ball to players who are standing...
a) seventy yards away
b) seventy centimetres away
c) seventy miles away

4. Once a goalie has made a decision about what they're going to do with a ball they must...
a) let their fellow players know
b) immediately change their mind
c) let their Mum know

5. During a match a goalkeeper must always be wearing a pair of...
a) professional goalkeeping gloves
b) big frilly knickers
c) massive specs

6. If a goalie has decided they're going to play the ball must let their team mates know by yelling…
a) KEEPER!
b) SAUSAGES!
c) BIG BUM!

7. If a goalie has decided to let their defenders play the ball they must yell…
a) AWAY!
b) FETCH!
c) BANANAS!

8. When a goalie is caught in 'no man's land' they have…
a) been indecisive, neither attacking the ball or getting themselves into a good 'shot-stopping' position
b) accidentally walked into the 'Ladies'
c) ended up on a World War One battlefield

9. As well as using their hands to pass the ball to team mates, goalies can also pass it…
a) by using their feet
b) by concentrating like mad and making it go on its own
c) by blowing on it really hard

10. If a keeper knows they aren't going to be able to catch a high shot they must…
a) punch the ball away
b) dance around in a circle
c) kneel down and cry

HOW DID YOU SCORE?

Work out how may times you answered A, how many times you answered B, and how many times you answered C. Then read your results below:

IF YOU ANSWERED MAINLY A

You might just have what it takes to be a top goalie. Keep practicing and you never know where you might end up!

IF YOU ANSWERED MAINLY B

While being a goalie might not be the best career path for you, ruling out football altogether doesn't have to be the answer. Try focus on becoming a striker or midfield player. If you're rubbish at that then it's time to move on!

IF YOU ANSWERED MAINLY C

Choose a career other than football - but perhaps not as a waiter or bomb disposal officer. You wouldn't want to drop anything!

CRUEL CRITICS

Playing in goal can be very testing indeed. And some of your critics can be very cruel if your performance isn't up to expectations. As David James found out!

HEE-HAW! MAVIS OUTPLAYS DAVID

It was 2004 and England were playing Austria in a qualifying game for the 2006 World Cup which was to be held in Germany. With David James playing in goal, England were winning 2-0 and it looked like they were on course for a World Cup place. After all, little Austria were only ranked 89th in the whole world! But then, in the 71st minute, David let in a free kick and, just two minutes later, he missed what critics said should have been a really easy save and the score went to 2-2.

Afterwards the Sun newspaper went nuts, calling David a donkey and printing his photo with donkey's ears superimposed on it. But that wasn't the end of it. The Sun went on to find a real donkey called Mavis, stuck it in front of a goal and rolled shots at it until it eventually flicked one away with its back legs.

WITH A HEADLINE READING:

SOME MORE GAMES THAT GOALIES WOULD RATHER FORGET

Being a goalie can sometimes be the best feeling in the world, saving goals and doing your team proud! However, it's usually the terrible games that people tend to remember!

DISASTROUS MISSES

During their World Cup qualifying match against New Zealand on 16th August 1981, Fiji's goalie managed to let in no less than 13 goals!

Final score: New Zealand 13 - Fiji 0

BUT THAT'S NOTHING COMPARED WITH THIS LOT...

- 24th November 2000:
  Iran 24 - The South Pacific island of Guam 0

- 14th February 2000: Kuwait 20 - Bhutan 0

- 9th April 2001: Australia 22 - Tonga 0

- 11th April 2001: Australia 31 - American Samoa 0

THAT'S THE SPIRIT!

Actually, in the group qualifying games in 2001, the American Samoans lost all four of their matches, letting in a total of

57 goals.

They didn't manage to put the ball into their opponent's net even once. However, it was reported that after their defeats, their ever-optimistic coach said,

"We're not too downhearted. We have to build from here. The only way is forward."

BRING ON THE STEP-LADDERS!

Of course, if you do play in goal, or any other position for that matter, it often helps to be tall, like six foot six inches Konstantinos Chalkias, who played in goal for Greece at the 2010 World Cup. However, if you aren't this tall, it can sometimes mean you're at a disadvantage. During the 1998 World Cup qualifying games, the Maldives played Iran. On average, the Maldives players were six inches shorter than the Iranians.

The Iranians beat them 17-0 and out of these 17 goals, ten were headers.

GO BANANAS!

Some goalies get a bit restless hanging about in goal. Such as the Peruvian goalkeeper Ramon 'El Loco' Quiroga who, during his team's 1978 World Cup game match against Poland, rushed off his line several times to tackle their players or clear the ball. One of these barmy charges got him a yellow card when he ran all the way into the Polish half to foul one of their players.

PUT ON A DAZZLING PERFORMANCE, OR JUST A DAZZLING KIT?

Some goalies go for wearing an outfit so psychedelically dazzling that it almost stops the opposing players in their tracks. Such as the ones regularly worn by the Mexican, keeper Jorge Campos. One of his most spectacular kits was the one, he wore at the USA World Cup in 1998.

HOW TO BE A WORLD CUP SOCCER ALL-ROUNDER

DRIBBLING

Some footballers are expert defenders, others great strikers and others good mid-field players. Some, seem to be good at everything: dribbling, defending, passing, shooting, the lot! One really useful skill for an all-rounder is dribbling. How much do you think you know about dribbling? Take this test and find out!

1 When dribbling, a footballer 'travels' with the ball by...

a) taking it on a world cruise

b) moving the ball around whilst controlling it with their feet, chest, knees and head

c) moving the ball around whilst controlling it with a giant magnet

2 Dribbling is often used to take the ball around...

a) a museum

b) the back of the bike sheds

c) an opposition player

3 Dribbling is mainly used when a team is on...

a) the attack

b) the coach home

c) holiday

4 When a player is dribbling the ball he has total control of...

a) the known universe

b) his bladder

c) the game

5 When you are dribbling the ball you are buying ...

a) some socks

b) time for your team mates to get into position

c) time for your team mates to go for a wee

6 If you can't dribble you are unable to...

a) let saliva trickle down your chin

b) play football properly

c) lick your own knees

7 The best dribblers in the world play as though the ball is part of their...

a) family

b) feet

c) small intestine

8 When you're dribbling the ball you must not look

a) like a big daft twerp

b) inside other peoples' cupboards

c) down

9 When you dribble you must touch the ball with...

a) every step

b) the tip of your nose

c) a flame thrower

10 Whilst dribbling you have to try to make the ball

a) cry

b) explode

c) do what you want it to do

PERFECT PENALTIES

A s a versatile, all-rounder you may be called upon to take a penalty kick. A penalty kick is a type of free kick that you take 12 yards (11 metres) out from the goal. Only the goalkeeper of the defending team is between you and the goal. The penalty kick was invented in 1891 by William McCrum, a Victorian textile tycoon and amateur goalkeeper.

THE BEST AND THE ERR . . . WORST!

England have the worst record in penalty shootouts of all the major football nations: a measly 17% success rate while Argentina have a whopping 73% success rate!

SO WHAT'S THE SECRET TO A PERFECT PENALTY? HERE ARE SOME TIPS:

1 Whatever you do, don't look at the goalkeeper. Crafty goalkeepers may attempt to distract you by talking to you, and moving around (waggling their bottoms at you, that sort of thing).

2 Stay focussed on what you are about to do. Do not start thinking about where you're going for your holidays, how big 'Space' is, or if you did your maths homework.

3 Ignore the yells of the opposition's fans who will be doing their best to distract you by yelling all sorts of insults.

4 Even if you are feeling tense and nervous you must try to remain calm.

5 Think positive thoughts and under no circumstances should you imagine missing the goal.

6 The goalkeeper will be watching you very carefully for signs of what you are planning to do, such as shooting high, shooting to the left. Try to avoid giving him clues as to your intentions by taking care where you place your feet and move your eyes.

7 Use power in your penalty kick. If you can kick at speeds of 80 miles per hour you can shoot the ball to the goal line in 500 milliseconds. To achieve this shot, shoot hard with your instep — from the laces (the laces of your boots, not your corsets). However, if it's 'precision over power' you want, use the inside of your foot.

8 Delay your shot. A delay of more than 13 seconds can unsettle the keeper (while a delay of more than two weeks will leave him clinically insane).

9 Aim the ball for the top right or top left corner of the net. This is the most difficult shot for the goalkeeper to stop. Though the top left or top right corner shots may have a 100% strike rate, they're very tricky to pull off and therefore you will be taking a bigger gamble if you try one.

10 Just before you take your shot, point at the sky behind the keeper and yell,

"CRIPES, PTERODACTYL!",

then blast in the ball.

SHOOTING, DEFENDING AND PASSING

What do you know about these other essential soccer all-rounder skills? Take the test and find out!

1 Before shooting, you should look to see if the goalkeeper has left...
a) his car lights on
b) town
c) a gap that you can exploit

2 When striking the ball you must keep your head...
a) ache tablets at the ready
b) down
c) tucked under your arm

3 When receiving a mid-air pass you must read...
a) the Bible
b) the flight, speed and direction of the ball
c) the flight, speed and direction of passing bees

4 When passing the ball to team mates it is important to know where they are by...
a) texting them
b) constantly looking around the pitch
c) hiring private detectives to stalk them night and day

5 When passing the ball you must pick...

a) a fight

b) your nose

c) someone to pass it to

6 If you lose the ball to an opponent...

a) it serves you right

b) try to win it back again

c) give up and go home

7 The safest way to pass a ball is with...

a) the inside of your foot

b) a police escort

c) it wrapped in cotton wool

8 Tackling is a soccer skill which demands...

a) a nice way with words

b) determination

c) body armour

9 When defending you must work to cause attackers to...

a) make a mistake

b) think twice about it

c) wish they'd never been born

10 When defending you must never give...

a) your name and address to strangers

b) blood

c) up

7 THE WORLD CUP'S WEIRDEST MOMENTS

PART TWO

Some more of the weirdest, wackiest and downright silly moments throughout World Cup history!

1 During the 1934 World Cup tournament the chief of the Italian Football Association, Dr Ottorino Barassi, was apparently so worried that the German army might steal the trophy that he kept it under his bed in a shoebox.

2 When, to everyone's astonishment, England were beaten by the USA 1-0 at the 1950 World Cup tournament, The New York Times newspaper apparently would not report the score because editors thought the whole thing was a hoax.

3 It is widely reported that at the 1966 World Cup final, English mid-fielder Nobby Stiles gave his false teeth to a pal and asked him to look after them, adding that if England did win, he would need them back very quickly for the press photo-shoot. However, his pal failed to get the teeth to him and a jubilant, dancing, gap-toothed Nobby appeared in the newspaper photos and became a footballing legend.

4 During the 1938 World Cup tournament, Brazilian player, Leonidas, tried to take off his boots and play in bare feet on a very muddy pitch during his team's game against Poland. The referee told him to put them back on so he did, scoring four goals in Brazil's 6-5 win.

5 Just before Italy's captain, Peppino Meazza, took a vital penalty in his team's 1938 semi-final against Brazil, the string on his shorts broke. So he took the kick holding them up with one hand. Then, as the ball sailed into the back of the net he let them drop around his ankles just as he was mobbed by his jubilant team mates.

6 When Juan Hohberg scored a late equaliser for Uruguay against Hungary in 1954, his delighted team mates jumped on him. When they finally climbed off him, they discovered he had passed out.

7 India withdrew from the 1950 World Cup because the officials wouldn't let them play in bare feet.

8 Romania's team for the 1930 World Cup was hand-picked by the King of Romania.

HOW TO SCORE A WORLD CLASS HEADER

Great soccer players use other parts of their body, including their heads to control the ball. World Cup wonder, 'Pele' once scored four headers in a single match. A record only beaten by his footballing dad who scored five in one match! If you want to score at least one brilliant World Cup class goal with what is known as an 'attacking' header, here's how to do it...

There are two key aspects to scoring a World Cup class header. The first is to overcome your fear of heading the ball. Quite sensibly, many people are frightened of heading the ball as it can be painful if done incorrectly. But with practise you can overcome this fear. The second is to 'smash' the ball with your head. Hitting the ball with your forehead is by far the least painful way of performing an attacking header.
Here's how to do it...

1 Keep your eyes on the ball the entire time it is travelling towards you. Get yourself in line with the flight of the ball.

2 Plant your feet. Not as you would 'plant' a tree, but just by keeping them firmly on the ground. This should give you the power to blast the ball past the goalkeeper. Keep your feet quite far apart so that your weight is centred evenly and bend your knees.

3 Lean back in order to build up the momentum for your 'killer' header. It's rather like bringing your foot back just before you kick the ball. Also keep your neck stiff.

4 If the ball is quite high in the air you will need to jump for it, especially if you are really tiny! You can do a one-footed or two footed take off (but never a three-footed one).

5 Bend back your upper body slightly then lunge forward to strike the ball. Use your back and waist muscles to move your head forward as quickly as you can in order to generate maximum power (but not so quickly that it actually leaves your shoulders).

6 Do not close your eyes. If you do, you could miss the ball completely and accidentally head the head of another player, or even the referee!

7 Keep your mouth closed, especially if you've got an extra big one, as the last thing you want to do is swallow the ball.

8 Make contact with the ball with the centre of your forehead. If you've got a really huge forehead, this will be a doddle! If you hit the lower half of the ball it will go up and if you hit the upper half it will go down. Aim the ball towards the ground (rather than at a passing aircraft). A 'ground' ball is harder for keepers to handle (especially if you've just smeared it with olive oil).

9 Extend your neck and keep your arms out at your sides for balance and protection from other players.

10 Once you have successfully put the ball in the back of the net run about pretending to be an aeroplane.

THE 'DIVING' HEADER

One really spectacular way to score a World Cup goal is with a 'diving' header. This is quite a dangerous thing to do, as when you are diving at the ball you could well end up diving at someone's boot, then have your head kicked into the goal rather than the ball. Also remember to land on your arms during the diving header (rather than your teeth).

If you are unable to overcome your fear of hitting the ball with your head and it does happen to come whizzing towards your head like a guided missile, the best thing to do is adopt the defensive tactic known as 'running away'.

NB this sort of things is not guaranteed to earn you the respect of your fellow team mates or fans.

Tip:

Practice your diving headers on a sandy beach. This way you will minimise the risk of injury (and also get a fabulous tan).

THREE WORLD CUP 'HEAD-ER' LINES

ot all footballers are keen to head the ball, even if it means missing the opportunity to score a cracking goal or pull off a brilliant save.

MIND MY HAIR-DO!

It was said that Uruguay's Pedro Petrone wouldn't head the ball when he played at the 1930 Uruguay World Cup because he didn't want to spoil his hairstyle.

DOCTOR'S ORDERS!

Apparently Brazil's Tostao wasn't allowed to head the ball when he played at the 1970 Mexico World Cup because he had a medical condition which could cause him to lose his sight if he did so.

BORISLAVOV AND HIS BOUFFANT!

Apparently Bulgaria's goalkeeper, Borislav Mickhailov, had just had a hair transplant, a real snip at a mere £25,000, and didn't want to spoil it by taking headers. In order to keep it perfect he took his hairdresser to the 1994 World Cup tournament in the USA.

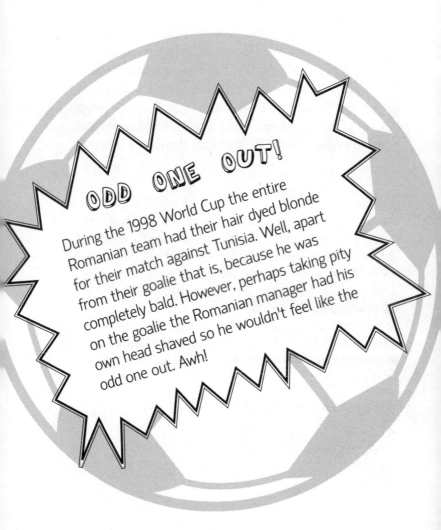

ODD ONE OUT!

During the 1998 World Cup the entire Romanian team had their hair dyed blonde for their match against Tunisia. Well, apart from their goalie that is, because he was completely bald. However, perhaps taking pity on the goalie the Romanian manager had his own head shaved so he wouldn't feel like the odd one out. Awh!

AW, REF!

REFEREE RIGHT OR WRONG

All football matches have to be controlled by a referee and two linesmen if they aren't going to involve a bit of player 'on-field naughtiness', or even descend into chaos. But referees aren't perfect and they sometimes make mistakes, which cause people to get very angry indeed. Here are three examples of very controversial World Cup match decisions by referees.

1 LET THE CAMERAS DECIDE

During the 2010 World Cup, England were 2-1 down against Germany when Frank Lampard took a shot at goal and hit the underside of the cross bar causing the ball to land a foot inside the goal line and rebound out of the net. The goal was disallowed by the referee, who said it had not crossed the line. In order to avoid situations like this in future, it has now been decided that a German camera-based, ball-tracking system called GoalControl will be used at the 2014 World Cup (and that the referees will all be given new spectacles).

2 OLIVE 'THE BOOK' THOMAS

During the game between Sweden and Brazil at the 1978 World Cup, Welsh referee Clive 'the book' Thomas, or Olive Thomas as he was called in the official programme, awarded a penalty to the Brazilians in the last moments of the match. The Brazilians took the penalty and scored. However, while the ball was still in the air, clock-watcher Clive blew his whistle for full time and the goal was disallowed. As he left the pitch the furious Brazilian fans bombarded Clive with coins. A very controversial decision! But remember, he was the referee who'd once waved a yellow card at a player as he was being stretchered off with a broken leg! No wonder he was known as 'the book'.

3 TIME KEEPING

It was the 1930 World Cup finals and France were trailing Mexico 1-0 in their second game of the tournament. A French forward had the ball and was about to boot it into the goal. However, as he prepared to do so the referee, Almeida Rego, blew his whistle for full time. Everyone, apart from Almeida, checked their watches and saw that there were still six minutes of play left!

HAVE YOU GOT WHAT IT TAKES TO BE A WORLD CUP REFEREE?

Think you've got what it takes to be an all star referee? Take the test and find out!

1. If a player commits a major foul, the referee gives him…
a) a red card
b) a Christmas card
c) a hug

2. To start or stop play, the referee blows…
a) a fuse
b) a trumpet
c) a whistle

3. **The linesmen are also known as...**
a) assistant referees
b) assistant librarians
c) assistant ballerinas

4. **If several players become involved in an angry scuffle the referee must...**
a) calm them down
b) yell, "FIGHT! FIGHT!" then join in
c) call the Fire Brigade

5. **It is essential for a referee to know...**
a) their ABC
b) the rules of football
c) how to make an absolutely delicious cream trifle

6. **Referees must give instructions in....**
a) a loud clear voice
b) Swahili
c) Cockney rhyming slang

7. When a 'free kick' is awarded to a player they are allowed to…
a) go on the world's best roller coaster without paying
b) kick the ball up as high as they can
c) take a kick at goal

8. When a free kick is taken, the ball must be…
a) hidden down the referee's shorts
b) stationary
c) really shiny

9. If a player commits an offence it is known as…
a) a foul
b) a chicken
c) a crying shame

10. A referee signals an indirect free kick by…
a) putting one arm straight up in the air
b) doing three cartwheels in quick succession
c) shouting, "Now look what you've gone and done!"

HOW DID YOU SCORE?

Work out how may times you answered A, how many times you answered B, and how many times you answered C. Then read your results below:

IF YOU ANSWERED MAINLY A

You could well become a world-class referee. But remember, your knowledge of the game must be backed up with clear, calm thinking, and the ability to make a decision and stick to it. And of course, you must have total self confidence when you're reprimanding extremely stroppy international soccer stars.

IF YOU ANSWERED MAINLY B OR C

Either forget refereeing as a career or sign up to a referee training course!

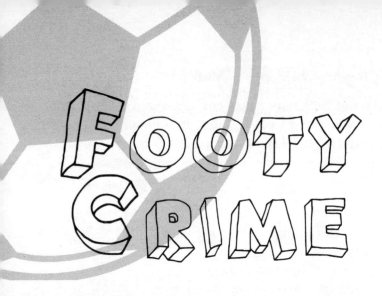

FOOTY CRIME

Sometimes injuries happen even when matches are being controlled by the referee. See if you can match the following offences to the players who committed them.

1. Spain 1982, France v West Germany:
Patrick Battiston niftily slipped the ball past this German goalie. But the keeper ignored it, and ended up knocking the French striker unconscious by smashing his hip into his face.

2. Mexico 1986, England v Argentina:
In the sixth minute of the second half goalie Peter Shilton and this striker went for a high ball. But instead of Shilton punching the ball away it was punched into the back of the net by the 'artful' Argentinian.

3. Germany 2006, Italy v France:
Italian player, Materazzi grabbed the shirt of this French striker. It is thought that he then said something unpleasant and was immediately knocked flat by a head butt.

4. Italy 1990, Germany v Holland:

This Dutch player was booked for a tackle on German player, Rudi Völler. As he got into position for the German free kick, he spat in Rudi's hair. Rudi complained to the referee and was booked as well. Next, the Dutch offender twisted Rudi's ear and stamped on his foot. After that both Rudi and the Dutch player were sent off. As they left the pitch the Dutchman spat in Rudi's hair again!

5. South Africa 2010, Spain v Holland:

This ferocious Dutch fouler gave Spanish midfielder Xabi Alonso a kung fu kick in the chest during the World Cup final. But Spain still went on to win the match 1-0.

Answers: ❶ Harald Schumacher ❷ Diego Maradona ❸ Zinédine Zidane ❹ Frank Rijkaord ❺ Nigel de Jong

Being the manager of a team at the World Cup or a TV commentator, is very demanding and requires a thorough knowledge of the game of football, not to mention a razor-sharp brain and the ability to simultaneously 'read' and assess a fast moving situation.

MANAGERS

Good soccer managers are absolutely crucial to a team's success. They have to be strong-willed, decisive and determined individuals who know how to deal with all sorts of characters. Alf Ramsey (1920-1999), who was in charge of the England team from 1963 to 1974 is a prime example.

THE BEST OF ALF

1 In 1966 Alf led England to their World Cup final victory in their 4-2 win over Germany.

2 Alf had been a footballer himself before taking over as manager of Ipswich and brilliantly leading them from the third division to win the F. A. Cup Final in 1961.

3 Alf came from a really poor background, growing up in a house in Dagenham that had no running water, no ~tricity and no inside loo.

4 Alf is said to have taken elocution lessons in order to sound posher than he was. But he always denied this.

5 When a reporter once asked Alf how the team were feeling he promptly told them, "There is great harmonium in the dressing room."

6 When England actually went to play in the World Cup in Mexico in 1970, Alf was worried that all those chillis and hot tamales would upset his players' stomachs. So in order to avoid this and ensure that the lads could enjoy the sort of nosh they were used to at home, Alf apparently had 63 kilos of burgers, 180 kilos of sausages, 136 kilos of fish and 10 cases of tomato ketchup shipped out to them from England.

7 After England beat Argentina 1-0 in the 1966 World Cup quarter-final, Alf is supposed to have described the Argentinians as acting like 'animals'. However, when all the statistics were totted up later it turned out that the Argentinian team had only committed 19 fouls, while Sir Alf's team had chalked a whopping 33 acts of soccer naughtiness.

8 When Geoff Hurst's third goal went in at the end of the 1966 World Cup final, it was plain to see that England had won. Quite naturally, everyone on the England bench went bananas, jumping up and down and shouting their heads off. All except for Alf that is. Apparently, he simply remained seated, calmly saying to England's ecstatic trainer, Harold Shepherdson, "Sit down and behave yourself Harold!"

TV COMMENTATORS

TV commentators sometimes come out with clangers.
Here's a couple of examples...

In 2006, one commentator told BBC TV viewers: "There's a real international flavour to this World Cup."

The Falkands War was being fought as the 1982 World Cup finals tournament opened and when doves were released at the end of the opening ceremony, Irish TV commentator, Jimmy Magee, said, "The symbol of peace... the pigeon."

OLYMPIC SIZZLER!

But really, being a TV commentator isn't an easy job. Especially if you were commentating on Madagascar's 2002 World Cup qualifier against Tunisia. Their team's names were: Ralison, Rasoanaivo, Razanfindrakota, Randrianoelison, Randrianaivo, Rrandriamarozaka, Ratsimihalona, Radonamaha, Rakotonbrabe, Radafison, Raharison. Oh, and their team coach was called Randriambololona. That lot must have been a real nightmare!

True or False?

Here are some more World Cup players' names that you might not have come across before! One of them has been made up but all the rest are genuine. See if you can pick out the imposter!

Robotti, Pardon, Neto, Bossio Grip, Chumpitaz, Knee, Gu Sang Bum, Bats, Albright, Titchy, Perfumo, Jelinek, Rats, Costly, Safari, Kiki, Rough, Van Heel, Grip, Kiss and Angel.

Answers: All true... apart from Knee!

89

MATCH THE TEAM TO THE NICKNAME

1 THE SOCCEROOS

2 LES ELEPHANTS

3 THE THREE LIONS

4 THE BLACK STARS

5 THE SUPER EAGLES

6 THE WHITE EAGLES

7 THE ALL WHITES

8 THE SCHWEIZER NATI

9 THE ORANJE

10 THE SAMURAI BLUE

A NIGERIA

B IVORY COAST

C NEW ZEALAND

D SWITZERLAND

E SERBIA

F JAPAN

G HOLLAND

H ENGLAND

I GHANA

J AUSTRALIA

WORLD CUP FOOTBALL JARGON Quiz

 Naturally, if you're going to be commenting on a TV game you'll need to be familiar with the language of football. Are you? Take the quiz below and find out!

1 A striker is…

a) someone who takes off all their clothes then runs across the pitch in the middle of a game

b) a footballer who refuses to play

c) a player whose job is to score goals

2 A volley is a…

a) low ground through which a river runs

b) stupid mistake

c) pass or shot which is struck before the ball touches the ground

3 A howler is a…

a) ridiculous mistake made by a player or referee

b) fan who never stops screaming

c) player who is always asking 'how' to do things

4 A dummy is…

a) a name given to the manager of a team who turned out to be a rubbish choice

b) what 'howlers' are given to keep them quiet

c) a player pretending to play the ball then actually letting it run past them

5 A chip is…

a) the nickname of top-scoring England player Charles 'Chip' Butty

b) something you wear on your shoulder after you brother steals the last chocolate biscuit

c) a shot hit with the intention of sending it over the keeper's head and into the goal

6 A kop is…

a) a uniformed officer whose job it is to keep the peace at a football match

b) a slang name for the spectators' stand behind the goal

c) to receive a reprimand: as in 'kop' a red card

7 A flick-on is…

a) when a player touches the ball with their head or foot to help it on its way

b) a quiffy hairstyle popular with England's World Cup winning 1966 team

c) what players say under their breath when they make a mistake

8 Cross is…

a) what managers get when their team aren't playing well

b) a player's delivery of the ball into the penalty area

c) something players have a quick pray to before they go up against a brilliant team

9 A boot boy is…

a) a young player whose job it is to clean the other players' boots

b) a young player whose job it is to sniff the other footballer's boots

c) a young player whose job it is to clean out the luggage compartment of the team manager's car

THE NUMBERS GAME

The other thing TV commentators love reeling off are numbers. Here are a few rather interesting ones for you to stun your pet cat or dog with.

15 The record number of World Cup goals scored by Brazilian forward Ronaldo.

56 Seconds into the game that is. That's how quickly José Batista of Uruguay was sent off in his team's match against Scotland at the 1986 World Cup tournament for his foul on Gordon Strachan.

25 The record number of World Cup match appearances by German footballer Lothar Matthaus.

11 Seconds into the game, was the time it took Turkey's Hasan Sukur to score the World Cup's fastest goal ever in his country's game against South Korea in the 2002 World Cup.

20 The record for most defeats suffered in World Cups, which is held by Mexico.

9 The number of World Cup tournaments won by countries from the continents of South America and European countries. In the 18 World Cup tournaments so far no other continent has produced a world champion country.

42 The age Cameroonian Roger Milla was at the USA World Cup in 1994 when he became the oldest goal scorer and the oldest player in World Cup history.

11 ONLY AT THE WORLD CUP!

STICKY SITUATIONS

With billions of people watching the World Cup on the telly and hundreds of thousands more actually attending the matches, and human nature being what it is, it's not surprising that all sorts of odd situations arise at this world-famous super-soccer tournament.

CURRY IN A HURRY!

World Cup games being held all over the planet means that fans have to travel. And sometimes when they do travel, they go to ridiculous extremes to ensure that they don't miss the 'comforts of home'. Ten fans from Scotland following their side during the 1998 World Cup in France obviously weren't too keen on French 'cuisine' so they phoned an Indian restaurant in Bournemouth and ordered themselves £600 worth of curry and lager! However, the restaurant informed them that it only did deliveries within a five mile radius, so the fans had to spend another £800 chartering an aeroplane to deliver their spicy nosh-up.

TWO WORLD CUPS WHERE ALL THE PLAY TOOK PLACE IN THE 'PENALTY AREA'S'

In 2002 France won the World Cup. And so did Brazil! But the French victory didn't take place at the World Cup tournament held in South Korea and Japan, which is where Brazil went on to victory. It happened at the Thailand Prison World Cup. The prison, which houses thirteen hundred foreign prisoners, set up its own World Cup tournament and eight teams took part including France, Germany, Italy, England and Nigeria. The French team defeated Nigeria on penalty kicks, 7–6.

THREE FAMOUS WORLD CUP WUFF-WUFFS

It's not only humans who get involved in making World Cup headlines. Dogs do to!

ONE MAN AND HIS DOG: 1962 WORLD CUP – CHILE

Part way through the match between England and Brazil, play was stopped when a dog joined in the game. A posse of players pursued the pesky pooch but were swiftly outclassed by its fancy footwork. But then, with the 'dogged' determination, which had made him a sporting hero, Jimmie Greaves got down on all fours and started to crawl towards the gobsmacked bow-wow. Mesmerised by the sight of England's third highest goal-scorer doing what looked like a lifelike impression of a big soppy spaniel, the dog froze in its tracks and Jimmie grabbed it by the scruff of the neck. He then handed it to an official and the game was restarted. But Jimmie now noticed that his shirt was very warm, very wet and very, very smelly! The dog had relieved itself all over his chest and Jimmie was forced to play the rest of the game reeking of dog wee.

Wrong sport mate - you're a boxer!

PICKLES: A 'FANS' BEST FRIEND'?: 1966 WORLD CUP - ENGLAND

While the security guards were having their break someone pinched the World Cup trophy. The thief was caught but the Cup couldn't be found anywhere and it looked like the tournament would have to be played without the trophy. But then a dog called Pickles saved the day when he found the Cup under a holly hedge. Pickles' owner was rewarded with £5,000 and Pickles received a year's supply of doggy treats.

A MANAGER'S BEST FRIEND?: 1978 WORLD CUP: ARGENTINA

This is a story about a different sort of 'wee' dog. Scotland were the only team from Great Britain which managed to qualify for this tournament. But, despite being tipped as possible winners, they only managed a 1-1 draw in their first game against Iran. At the press conference afterwards, their miserable manager, Ally Mcleod, was just saying, "I've few friends left now," when a cute brown dog scampered up to him. The quick-thinking coach wittily added, "In fact the only friend I have now is this wee brown dog," and he put out his hand to stroke the dog. The dog bit him.

Och ya bonny wee dog!

GLOSSARY

boot boy A young player whose job it is to clean the other players' boots

Calcio Meaning 'kick' in Italian, this is the name used for football played in Italy

chip A shot hit with the intention of sending it over the keeper's head and into the goal

chloroform A clear liquid that can be inhaled and used as an anaesthetic (it is poisonous, so is no longer used for this purpose)

civil war A war between citizens of the same country

consecutive One straight after another

cross A player's delivery of the ball into the penalty area

decapitated Having one's head cut off

dictator Someone who rules with total power over their country, often cruelly

diving header Diving towards the ball with your whole body then heading it during your dive

dribbling Moving the ball past another player using continuous small touches

dummy A player pretending to play the ball then actually letting it run past them

Fascist A dictatorial leader (someone who rules with total power over their country, often cruelly)

flick-on When a player touches the ball with their head or foot to help it on its way

hat-tricks Three goals scored by one person in a single game

howler A ridiculous mistake made by a player or referee

Jabulani balls New footballs designed by Adidas that were used for the 2010 World Cup in South Africa

kop A slang name for the spectators' stand behind the goal

linesman Official who assists the referee from the sideline

no man's land When a goalkeeper is 'stuck' because they have neither attacked the ball nor got themselves into a good defensive position

penalty area Also known as the box; the rectangular area around the goal

penalty kick A free kick on the goal that can only be defended by the goalkeeper (awarded to the attacking team when someone has fouled an attacking player in the box)

penalty shootouts Used at the end of a tournament game to decide which team should win the game in the event of a tie; teams take it in turns to take penalty kicks (up to five kicks each) until one team has won by scoring more goals than the other

plinth A heavy base or platform

striker A player whose job it is to score goals

superstitious Believing that certain events or actions will bring good or bad luck for other unrelated events

volley A pass or shot which is struck before the ball touches the ground

INDEX

FURTHER INFORMATION

BOOKS

Fitter, Faster, Funnier Olympics by Michael Cox (A & C Black, 2012)

50 Soccer Skills by Jonathan Sheikh-Miller (Usborne, 2008)

2014 FIFA Word Cup Brazil Official Book by Jon Mattos (Carlton Books Ltd, 2014)

Big Match Manager by Tom Sheldon and Nathan Burton (Bloomsbury 2004)

WEBSITES

FIFA
http://www.fifa.com

Kidnetic
www.kidnetic.com

Change for life
http://www.nhs.uk/Change4Life/Pages/change-for-life.aspx

Michael Cox
www.michaelcox.info

Fitter, Faster, Funnier Olympics!

The Olympic games are one of the most famous sporting events of all time. From unbelievable tales of triumph to amazing facts about countless Olympic athletes, Fitter, Faster, Funnier Olympics is a hilarious guide to the Olympics past and present. Packed full of hilarious illustrations, fantastic quizzes and head scratching brain teasers. Plus find out if you've got what it takes to become an Olympic athlete!

£4.99

978-1-4081-655-84